# COLLEEN'S
## Collection of Poetry

# COLLEEN'S Collection of Poetry

By Colleen Kim

ASA PUBLISHING CORPORATION
An Innovative Outsource Book Publishing Hybrid

ASA Publishing Corporation
25 S. Monroe Street, Monroe, Michigan 48161
*An Accredited Publishing House with the BBB*
www.asapublishingcorporation.com

---


Book Title: Colleen's Collection of Poetry
Date Published: 05.26.2023 / Edition 1 *Trade Paperback*
Book ID: ASAPCID2380874
ISBN: 978-1-960104-10-6
Library of Congress Cataloging-in-Publication Data

This book was published in the United States of America.
Great State of Michigan

# Table of Contents

# COLLEEN'S
# Collection of Poetry

By Colleen Kim

# 02.02.11

# POETRY – IN THE BEGINNING

About a week after my mastectomy, everyone I would see
would ask, "When was your surgery?"
I knew they were just filling out their charts,
or possibly genuinely concerned.
So after about the fifteenth inquirer
I sat down and wrote:

February second, two thousand eleven,
my right boob went to heaven.
Whether it was its destiny
or its cancerous fate,
I don't know,
but I hope it's waiting for me at the pearly gate.

# 2010 TORNADO

How does one sleep through a
tornado doing devastation to your
yard uprooting trees
and scattering debris
and yet two lives untouched, unscarred?

Several weeks of clean up
from many helpful hands.
We got it back
with the help of Jack
and many groups, strangers, and friends.

God's hand of protection was on us.
Through the darkness he kept us in sight,
and now I know
for he did show
He was there on that dreadful night.

# A SPECIAL BOY

Yes. It's true I'm in love with him.
Each day without him is very grim.
I wait impatiently for him to call,
and sometimes I climb the wall.
He's very kind, but much too shy,
and then I wonder why
he doesn't even hold my hand
even though we've been out time and time again.
He makes me want to keep on living
I can't quit cause my heart won't stop ticking.
My one big question, is this really true love?
'Cause he never shows a sign that he loves me enough.

# AN APPLE

An apple for my teacher,
not quite as perfect as it ought to be– the apple–not the teacher,
was picked from an imperfect tree. Could say this apple for my teacher was rotten from skin to core–
the apple–not the teacher
as was stated just before. But this apple for my teacher
will probably be thrown away–
the apple–not the teacher
has seen a better day!

# ANGEL

You were there for me in my darkest hours
to encourage and gently guide.
Each survivor has been blessed
to have had you by her side.
God sends us angels,
and you are one of his.

# BECKY'S MASTER'S DEGREE CARD

'Twas the week before Christmas
and Becky earned herself a master's degree.
All those around her
would have to agree.
This accomplishment is next to none.
We wish her congrats
for a job well done.

We're proud of you!

Love, Mom and Dad

# BOOBLESS IN OHIO

## Like Sleepless in Seattle

Well, I bowed down to making a decision I didn't want.
I have no self-worth.
I used to hate things about me.
(Like wanting people to understand me and accept me.)
Now I hate me.
Doctor Lininger is going to chop off my right breast
which she wanted me to "ok,"
and like a good little patient
I did–do I mean it? No–I have no choice–or so they say.
I don't want to live as a freak.
My body cut, mutilated, and left disfigured.
I pray she cuts a vein and I die on the table.
How horrific you say–but how horrific being part of a woman.
That's right–it used to be by figure–as overweight as it was,
it was a figure–my figure.
So much for saving the ta-tas, as the bumper sticker reads,
now I'm not whole,
but there is a hole,
a hole no kind words can fill.
Put on a smile and say positive things so everyone
thinks everything is ok–it's not–I would rather be dead.

# CANCER JOURNEY

How much physical and emotional pain can she endure
before they find a medical cure.
We race and walk thru our journey miles,
sometimes in tears and often elusive smiles.
Not knowing what tomorrow has in store,
but we know the new normal won't be as it was before.
Do not worry–come what may
Take a deep breath, live this day.

# Card Given to Radiation Team

# At UTMC at Last Visit

Here's what I'm gonna miss . . .
Scanning my green card and waiting my turn,
hoping and praying I won't get burned.
Watching my weight go up each week–I'll miss that a lot.
Cold hands and colored markers on my tattooed dots
lying distorted on the hard metal table.
Trying to get up—and not being able.
Having my left boob taped to my arm
to hold it down so it won't get harmed,
but most of all I'll miss seeing each of you every day.
This was kind of fun in a weird kind of way.

# CHRISTMAS CRISIS

Had your fill of dropping glass sparkling balls?
Running frantically through crowded malls?
Tired of hearing "Jingle Bells," and "Deck the Halls?"
Sounds like you have a Christmas crisis.

Does your mistletoe keep falling down?
Has your Christmas cheer turned to a frown?
And all your friends are visiting out of town?
Sounds like you have a Christmas crisis.

How 'bout that fake scraggly tree?
Or trying to explain how a fat man slides down the chimney?
Shucks, it's not even safe to sit on Santa's knee.
This is really a Christmas crisis.

I throw on my chenille robe–so what if it's torn.
Wow! It's already Christmas morn.
Kids are up. Honk! Little Jimmy got a horn.
This is a Christmas crisis.

By looking at the boxes we sure are blessed–
if you base it on the papered mess.
Well, we're off to church–let's all get dressed.
No time for a Christmas crisis.

We all sing songs of the silent night
How the baby Jesus was born under a beaming star light.

I think I've forgotten the Christmas story and have lost sight;
Joseph, Mary, and Jesus never had a Christmas crisis.

# CONSOLING MY FRIEND

I said a prayer today
for my friend Kay,
that if I should go away
it would be ok.
She knows I couldn't stay
to watch my hair turn to gray,
but as my body does die and decay
my spirit goes home–it knows the way,
and it will be ok.

# CORDIAL INQUIRIES

People ask, “How’s your cancer?”
And this is my sarcastic answer:
“Cancer–it has gone away
but lymphedema and other problems
are here to stay.”

Everyday I exercise, massage
and wear a compression sleeve,
and look at my missing breast and grieve.

How could I have been so dumb
to make a choice that has left me numb.

# DEMENTIA

If I should get dementia, don't listen to what I say.
Well you can listen–some things might be funny.
But my experience is that the words and phrases are hurtful (whether true or not).
I guess the most hurtful, painful thing is to see someone that you love fade from this reality into their own world.
Usually not letting you in–being negative and not allowing you care for and love them.
All I can say at this time is I'm sorry. I know you love me and hopefully this part of the journey "home" will be quick.
Be patient, for this will not last long. Then I will be in heaven–my mind, body and spirit shall be renewed.

Amen

# DID YOU EVER . . .?

Pretend that you were someone you weren't?
Ask a stupid question?
Forget a word in the middle of a sentence?
Listen to a love song and think it was written about you?
Wonder what your purpose is?
Feel alone in a crowd?
Just want to give up?

# EVEN ME

A poem I wrote for a G.A. ceremony at F.B.C.

Who are the G.A.'s and what do we do?
Just a moment of your time, and I'll explain G.A.'s to you.
Some of us are young, and just starting out,
learning about missions and what missionaries are all about.
Others of us have learned for many years
about mission work both far and near.
So, whether your mission field is in Perrysburg or far away,
our G.A. leaders have taught us how to serve, to give, and how to pray.
God isn't particular who he chooses to use.
You don't need to be a missionary to spread the good news.
Yes–even I, as a little girl,
can share God's love in this great big world!

# EVEN MORE

He loves you when you're happy.
He loves you when you're sad,
and yes, He even loves you
when you get angry and mad.
He loves you when you're behaving,
and even when you're bad.
To tell you the truth,
He loves you ever so much more
than even your mom and dad.

# GIVE ME A CLUE

I have no purpose in my life.
I'm not a daughter, sister, mom, or wife.
Why am I here? What am I to do?
Please tell me 'cause I don't have a clue.

# GOD IS FOREVER

Flowers wilt and die.
Clouds drift swiftly by.
Leaves fall down.
Grass withers and turns brown.
Snow melts on hardened ground.
Stones crumble,
mountains tumble,
but God is forever.

# GONE CHILD

Your heartbeat was strong,
and in an instant your heartbeat was silenced.
Where is the child that never got to cry?
That never was held by those who loved him?
What color was his hair and eyes?
What name shall I call you?
My heart aches from the emptiness.
My arms will never hold you.
I will never hear you say, "I love you, Mimi."
And God looked down and saw the helpless child,
and put him in the palm of His hand
and caressed him with His unending love.

# HOME

A house becomes a home
when tiny handprints are on the walls,
and the sounds of laughter and giggles
are heard from down the hall.
When the front door swings off its hinges
from people running in and out.
A home–and not just a house–
is what living is all about.
So the next time something breaks
and you think it's time to sell–
just remember all the memories
in this home where we all have dwelled.

# I AM A ROCK

I speak to you, falls,
as an innocent rock
brought to shore with your great strength.

From here I see
the other (more powerful rocks)
which you are now, too, trying to push away
from where they have rested for so many years.
With the force of your current
so strong that the water is turning white with enthusiasm and
vigor.

All you are really doing
is cleansing the rugged surface
so it may shine with victory and triumph
as the sun beats upon it.

Exhausted, but never ending,
you move downstream
only to follow what before you has failed.
Go calmly but proud–for you have tried . . .

# I AM THANKFUL FOR-

I am thankful for
hazy rays of sunlight
shining through the golden leaves
yet clinging on the trees . . .
The shimmering grass
glistening until footprints melt
the frost into the heavy morning dew
collecting upon your shoes . . .
The dancing of falling leaves
scattering as you shuffle through . . .
The cleansing breath of the fresh crisp autumn air . . .
The quiet stillness of nature's beauty . . .
The endless array of colors
from gold to harvest brown . . .
So quickly has passed the long hot summer days
and soon the dark cold winter will be upon us . . .
Yet time stands still for a moment
as we try to capture the beauty of this season.
I am thankful.

# I BECAME THE UNIBOOBER

One morning I woke up at about four a.m.
I couldn't sleep.
I sat on the edge of my bed and looked down at my body.
What a freak!

The heroic words people would say rang in my head.

Warrior. Fighter. Survivor.

These names did not describe how I felt.

Then my mind went to overcoming the war with cancer and for a moment I became a superhero.
Most superheroes are freaks.

Examples: Superman, $6,000,000 Man, The Fly, Hulk, Spiderman, etc.
Likewise, I, the Uniboober, am a freak–fighting cancer.

This is when I came up with an idea for a comic book cover:
The Uniboober.
Pink cape, pink mask, radiation sword, chemo knife.
Standing on top of the world.

# I NEVER GOT TO SAY GOODBYE

There are several people that have come and gone and I never got to say goodbye.

The most recent was my grandson, Luca.

I never met him, saw him, held him, touched him, heard his cry, or smelled his baby skin,

and I never got to say goodbye.

After losing my grandson, I also lost my granddaughter Baela, 6,
grandson Elliott, 3,
and Luca's twin sister, Lucy, 18 months.

These three did not die, but rather I have been prohibited to see or talk to them. And I never got to say goodbye.

So now before I forget, let me say goodbye, in case I don't get a chance to later.

# I WALK AWAY
# AND HOMEWARD BOUND

Walking down the lonely road
between the fields of autumn gold
from far away I can barely see
the outline of an empty tree.
I can see the bridge where I often sit
and remember things I cannot forget.
I recall the love that there never was.
To me they were true, to him they were false.
I look out over many miles and wish I could be
anywhere far from Lime City.
To be able to be on my own, independent, and all alone.
I want no friends, for friendship causes pain.
So I live the rest of my life in vain.
I'd forget the past and start again
with not a trace of tears–only a grin.
This isn't possible for I am trapped
in a society I cannot adapt.
I come from my dream to face reality
that I have to be what God wants me to be.
As I walk back the sun does set
and I go home with deep regret.

# I WAS SENT ON A JOURNEY

God sent me on a journey.
I didn't want to go.
It seemed I traveled alone,
and the destination I did not know.
But when I held my head up
I saw there were many that had gone before.
Walking right beside me,
and now I'm just one more.
So many steps we've taken,
so many more ahead.
Sometimes glancing backward . . .
Have you ever questioned where He has led?

# I'M STUCK IN A DARK PLACE

I'm stuck in this dark place.
Even though the sun is on my face,
there's a mistake I made that I can't erase.
It's not getting better with the passing of days,
or even with uplifting words that someone will say
that everything will be ok.
I'm stuck in this dark place.

I don't think I'm supposed to be here anymore.
When you don't have anything to be living for,
how can depression give God praise?
Sitting–wasting all my days.

# LEAVING

The one that stays am I
waving to the one leaving
and saying goodbye.
Pulling at my heart
trying not to cry,
but pools of tears fill my eyes.
My fingers blotting
my cheeks to dry.
. . . and you have gone . . .
The one that stays am I.

# LIFE UPON A STAGE

The curtains are left open on that stage, where the murder had occurred,
and the floor is still stained where Clarissa's blood once poured.
The setting is dark and mysterious and the stage is left alone.
Once ovations and applause filled this forgetful crowd for actors that will never be known.
Each person played a character on the morbid stage,
and read the slowly ending life of their character as they turned each page.
When that play was over, the lights dimmed away,
and life was over for each character whose name was in that play.
The long, velvet curtain slowly ended each character's life
which struck the audience with a piercing knife.
The cast walked toward the applauding group to take their final bow,
but today the audience has gone away, and the seats are empty now.

# LIVE THIS DAY

How much physical and emotional pain can she endure
Before they find a medical cure?
We race and walk through our journey miles.
Sometimes in tears and often elusive smiles.
Not knowing what tomorrow has in store,
but we know the new normal won't be as it was before.
Do not worry–come what may.
Take a deep breath and live this day.

# LYNN'S B-DAY CARD

'Twas the night before your birthday and all thru the kitchen,
the hormones were flying and the crew was a-bitchin'.
But suddenly, what did I see?
A team of eight ladies as busy as bees;
Jan pushing a cart and telling a joke.
Sheila trying to cool down and out for a smoke.
Carol reading a recipe and mixing her cake.
Amber cupping up applesauce and making the shakes.
Janet putting on gloves and washing the dishes.
Robyn garnishing lemons on the baked fishes.
Sue filling the trays and checking her list.
Colleen getting a tub of dirty dishes and not breaking her wrist.
We're all different, but one thing is true,
we all wish our boss, "Happy birthday to you!"

# MOTHER

Father told me long ago when I was a child
of your temper, and your laughter, with your hidden smile.
You taught us to be church goers and how to say our prayers,
when we children went to bed up the towering stairs.
You punished us–but oh so fairly,
I thank you today for treating us squarely.
You always knew what was unfair and just,
except the time we were all together–then you left us.
And now as I look at your picture hanging lonely on the wall,
I wonder if you had a friend in this world at all.
Looking at your pale eyes and your long, dark, hair piled on your head,
he says that I should forget you now, now that you are dead.
How could I forget walking behind you on that dismal day?
When God chose you to leave our home, and go along your way.
People asked, "How's your family?" And here's what we'd reply,
"Lonesome, cause Mom has gone to heaven and she didn't say goodbye."
I'm keeping the family all together so when we meet again
it'll be the same happy family as it was then.
Memories of you will last forever for I've grown up to be
the perfect maiden of our house. "Father's sweet young lady."
It reminds him of the way you worked about the house–
sweeping, washing, sewing, cooking–as quiet as a mouse.
I get along fairly well without your helping hand.
I only wish that you were here on this earthly land.

It's not the same without a mother into which you can confide,
If you failed, but did your absolute best, your mother knows you tried.
Each day I think of you and often start to weep–
that you had to go into that dark and everlasting sleep.
But in our hearts and minds you linger–I guess you always will.
Until we're resting right beside you on that old quiet hill.

# MY BABY IS HAVING A BABY

I held you in my arms–just yesterday.
You learned to walk and you were on your way.
Looking and wanting to go outside,
I felt the heart strings slowly untie.
Soon you were going to school and meeting new friends . . .
The phone rang and it was a boy named Ben.
Off to college and out the door,
it was never quite the same as it was before.
Slowly maturing and growing independent from me
is what a mother raises her child to be.
You fell in love and said, "I do."
Two lives whose love each day grew.
And in your arms you'll hold your little one
and then their story will have begun.

# NICOLE - A COUNSELOR

You were there for me in my darkest hours
to encourage and gently guide.
Each survivor has been blessed
to have had you by her side.
God sends us angels,
and you are one of his.
A woman of virtue,
a friend who we will sincerely miss.

# NO ONE TO FOLLOW

All my life I've waited,
for this day to come to an end.
Now that it's over–well over,
I wish it never began.

We walked by the seashore.
We walked hand in hand.
You told me that it's over, to go my separate way–
but I followed you, tracing your footsteps in the sand.

The sun began to set, bouncing on the waves.
I looked straight ahead–never glancing behind.
I suddenly turned around and you were gone.

Just like the sun
that will never rise again;
just like me,
who will never love again.
I am alone,
all alone.

# UH-OH

Excuse me. Have you seen my cleavage?
Oh my goodness–I've lost my cleavage.
Something is terribly wrong.
This cannot be.
My right boob is gone.
Where could it have gone?
It can't just get up and walk away.
Wait a minute.
I bet it was that thing I've heard about.
I think it goes by the name of cancer.
One day everything is hunky dory,
and the next, this cancer thing appears.
And your life is not the same.

# ONE AUGUST DAY

One August day,
I made my way,
down a long, long, narrow road.
Between fields of corn
and acres of beans,
grew various woods of green.
Every so often there was a bird house though no bird did I see.
Just a cardinal hiding atop a group of bushes
singing his song for me.
The katydid and cricket joined,
in one melodious song.
I stopped to listen for a moment,
but I didn't sing along.
This path that I had followed
led me to a farm.
An old, large house, a barn, some sheds
captured a solitude of charm.
So now I journey back to you to tell you what I've seen.
That God and I slowed down today
to have this time–
just Him and Colleen.

# OOPS

Mistake I made.
The price I paid.

# OPPOSITES

This was a book I made for Baela for her first birthday present. It was written and illustrated by Mimi.

up down

left right

happy sad

day night

short tall

fat thin

sit stand

out in

little big

stop go

walk run

fast slow

empty full

young old

hard soft

hot cold

# OXYGEN BLIPS

Suck it up.

I can't breathe,
and my name is not
George Floyd.

See me?
I'm the one with the hose in her nose.

D.M.E. accessories make my outfit.

# PERSISTENCE

I keep on trying
to no avail.
I keep on trying,
and all I do is fail.
But I haven't failed
if I keep on.
Persistence is the energy
until the attempts are done.

# RETIREMENT

Days go by slowly.
Nights go by even slower.
Much too far away is tomorrow,
and the yesterdays flash by quickly,
and suddenly it's today again.

# SURRENDER TO THE LORDSHIP OF JESUS CHRIST

Jesus, Savior, Messiah, friend,
are all names easy for me to say,
but to call you Lord is difficult
for my pride gets in the way.

I have yet to learn to surrender.
I have trouble being humble and meek.
My life's filled with good intentions,
but seldom your will I seek.

How can you develop a Christ-like spirit
in a strong-willed child like me,
when I refuse to release control
and set my spirit free?

My prayer is to be more amiable
and to let you have your way.
Then I could call you Lord of my life,
and Lord would be easy to say.

# TALKING TO WATER

Let me ask you this, Great Lakes–

When man drinks your water
does he taste
or only quench his thirst?

When he washes his hands in you
does he feel you
or merely cleanse away the dirt?

When he rides upon your waves
does he feel you move
or only notice himself going forward?

And if he tried to walk upon you
would he drown
or float
from confidence that he hasn't taken advantage of you?

# THANKSGIVING POEM

I'm sitting at home a little stir crazy.
You can bet your dad is working
and not feeling lazy.
So here I am writing the poem of Thanksgiving,
being thankful that my children are all well and living.

There may be no sun,
but they are out for a run,
doing something healthy together that's fun.

My kids are all safe in the state of New York.
The turkey is cooked so pick up your fork.
Today is Thanksgiving, and I know what I'm thankful for;
having wonderful children and a grandson,
but I'd like some more.

# THE CARPENTER'S SON

Just another day in the carpenter's shop,
watching the men as they sawed and chopped.
As a young boy he could hear the echoing sound
of the hammers striking nails as they were pound.
Rather ironic with what was to be–
that this carpenter's son would be nailed to a tree.
So the next time you pick up a hammer and you give it a swing,
remember the carpenter's son,
and the nails that pierced the hands and feet of the King of
Kings.

# THE CRY OF A TROUBLED HEART

I want to be alone,
but I don't want you to leave.
My heart is filled with pain,
and my spirit soars with grief.

A raging war within,
though not visible from what people see,
covered up with put-on smiles
so no one knows the real me.

I'm afraid to be open and true
even though you know my heart.
The fear of your rejection
is tearing me apart.

# THE DANCING LADY

Acrylic painting, small wire sculpture, large garden wire sculpture

Sometime soon,
I'll dance again.
I'll laugh again.
I'll remember happiness.
Take my hand and
let me hear the
joyful music.

# THE FALLEN WALL

Sometimes I build a wall around myself,
and seclude myself from the outside world.
Letting no one touch me
and not letting myself reach out to anyone–
not even through the cracks and crevices that may occur and grow in time.
But then someone comes along,
climbs the wall,
looks down on me,
and holds out his hand to me.
I look up,
extend my arm,
and climb out of the hole in which I have been living
and been calling my world.
It seems now that again I have started to build the wall.

# THE LOSS OF WOMANHOOD

The essence of my womanhood is now packed up and sitting in a bag,
various sizes of feminine pads and bras with a 44C tag.
I grieve the loss of the woman in the mirror in which I once knew well . . .
I don't know this woman–
she's mutilated and disfigured,
like a monster from the depths of hell.
A freakish pose–a glimpse I see
as she begins to undress.
What man is there that longs for her
to love, touch, kiss, and caress?

# THE MISERIES OF MY COLD

I have a cold.
I can hardly breathe.
I cough, sniffle, and then–I sneeze.
I blow my nose.
I take an aspirin,
and down my throat cough syrup goes.
When will it end?
I hope today!
My head won't be plugged up,
and I'll be ok!

# THE ORANGE PANEL TRUCK

Daddy had an orange panel truck.
It ran pretty good.
He installed garage doors
back when garage doors were made of wood.

We'd ride around the countryside.
He'd say, "I put that one in." Momma would give a nod.
Daddy would give a grin.

It was hard work–long hours
sunup to sundown,
driving that orange panel truck
around Ohio to every small town.

He'd climb the ladder–tighten the bolts
and whistle a little tune,
wipe the sweat off his brow with a handkerchief
and stop for lunch at noon.

It seemed everyone knew my daddy.
They all called him Spike,
all the people from Lime City
and down Fremont Pike.

# THE PROTESTORS

What is this world coming to?
When people do the things they do? Students riot and carry signs
hoping to change these worldly times.
They can't accept periodical recall of troops
so they assemble on campuses and protest in groups. The fuzz can't stop them for you see,
the radicals cry out, "police brutality!" Will this commotion help us end the war, and bring back peace as it was before?

The 60's
Vietnam!

# THE WAITING ROOM

There are seven people sitting in a blue
four-cornered room.
Two reading the newspaper.
Two sleeping in a chair in the corner.
One nervously biting his fingernails.
One lighting a cigarette.
and I am the seventh, writing.
The people I see; each different in their own way–but all await.
Disturbed not by the sounds of the turning pages,
sighs and coughs,
or maybe the occasional squeak of the leather chair.
Then suddenly all eyes are focused on another person entering the room.
I, wondering what he will do to pass the waiting minutes of time.

# THE WHORE

Woman what ya doin'?
Who ya think you're foolin'?
With your come-on eyes
and bag of lies.
Can't ya see it's your life you're ruinin'?
When ya gonna get wise?

So many men you've had.
They come and treat ya bad.
They treat ya like dirt.
Oh, it really hurts.
Sometimes makes ya mad
that ya gotta be such a flirt.

The fancy clothes,
their turned-up noses,
puts ya in your place.
You're only a disgrace to the female race,
but that's the way it goes.
It's a reality ya got to face
to keep up with the pace.

# THREE MEANINGLESS WORDS

You told me, "I think I love you."
I say to you, "Don't think.
Know and be sure you love me.
And if you do,
you won't have to say it,
because I'll know . . ."

# TO BE FOUND

A child searches aimlessly through a gathered crowd
for his mother, but the voices are too loud,
and his crying is smothered.
Are we too proud to be bothered?

Can't we reach out and grasp his tiny hand?
If only as a friend
helping him to understand
that in the end
he will see this as a man.
Together, few were the moments we had time to spend.

Suddenly from his saddened eyes a tear
trickles and then flows down his cheek.
His face of fear is patterned by the drops that quickly begin to streak.
If only his mother were here.
She would listen to the words he longs to speak,
"I've found a friend in a crowd of strangers."

# TO: YOU FROM: GOD

My Christmas gift to you
is not wrapped in festive foil and bows,
but came as a meager babe
wrapped simply in swaddling clothes.
He's not placed under a Christmas
tree with tinsel and lights all aglow,
but rather in a dark and dirty stable
where even the oxen bow low.
The gift I give to you
is the same that was given to me.
That this baby whose name is Jesus
30 years later was crucified upon a tree.
God's given to us the gift of eternal life
for all who confess and believe.
But a present isn't a present
until the recipient does receive.
You see my gift was sent from heaven
and not some store bought thing.
So you can't exchange or take it back
It's perfect–as is the King of Kings.

# TWO FRIENDS OF MINE

## (Oil pastel on velour)

I had two friends–one stayed–one went away.
I remember it was a cold and icy day.
The friend that stayed helps me not to forget
my friend that left. That choice I regret.
They were so well rounded–a bouncing pair
and now one of them is gone; it’s not there.
The three of us were not perfect
‘cause perfect is not me,
but we were as close to being whole
as long as we were three.

# UNIQUE SNOWFLAKES

One Christmas snowflake
now gliding through the air.
How unique and special!
Its beauty is too rare.

Two Christmas snowflakes
dancing through the air.
How unique and special!
What a lovely pair.

Three Christmas snowflakes
twirling through the air.
How unique and special!
Our warm wishes and love we share.

*2014(?) A Christmas poem that describes at this time my 3 children; Jenn (1) Becky and Ben (2) and Randy, Annie, Kaden (3)*

# WASTING

I don't think I'm supposed to be here anymore.
When you don't have anything to be living for.
How can depression give God praise?
Sitting–wasting all my days.

# WE'RE GETTING OLD

Age spots, wrinkles,
gray hair, leaky tinkles,
aches and pains,
varicose veins,
saggy parts,
slip out farts,
loss of hearing, sight, and mind.
To the old, God's not kind.

# WHEN YOU ARE CLOSE, I FEEL LOVE

Many people I have loved,
but not as much as you.
You make me warm when I am cold
just by being near.

When you are close enough–
I hold out my hand to you,
and look straight into your eyes,
and you seem to know.

You embrace my body
as if never to let me go,
and then I'm sure
you're all I need.

# WINTER HAS COME UPON US AND IT'S TOO LATE

It's too late to smell the flowers.
It's too late to lie in the grass.
So quickly passed the hours,
and now the winter shadows are cast.

Even the leaves have fallen.
Their colors turned past brown.
The winter wind is callin'
for them to be placed onto the frozen ground.

But the blue skies still appear,
and the white clouds they drift by.
The winter crispness is here
as the warm summer breezes die.

The snow covers the earth in white,
and trees are dark and bare.
So quickly comes the night,
and the dark and stillness are everywhere.

The winter has touched both our hearts
and left us bitter and cold.
For we've drifted so far
apart it's you I can no longer hold.

It’s too late to turn to you.
It’s too late for you to turn to me.
No matter what you say or do
you are you–I am I–and we are no longer we.

# WRITING A POEM ON PERSISTENCE

The assignment was to write a poem
on persistence,
which turns out to be rather hard.
But I'll keep trying my best
and thinking of words,
so I might win a fifty dollar gift card.

www.ingramcontent.com/pod-product-compliance
Lightning Source LLC
LaVergne TN
LVHW010841120826
845149LV00017B/3417

* 9 7 8 1 9 6 0 1 0 4 1 0 6 *